Little People, BIG DREAMS™
MINDY KALING

Written by
Maria Isabel Sánchez Vegara

Illustrated by
Roza Nozari

Frances Lincoln
Children's Books

Little Vera Mindy Chokalingam was the second
child of an Indian couple who fell in love in
Africa and moved to America before she was born.
They called her Mindy after a sitcom they both loved.

At school, Mindy didn't fall in love with math or science, but she could remember every word of the movies she loved. She would take a notebook to the cinema and write down the lines that made her laugh the most.

But at the end of every movie, Mindy was always left feeling that she was the only Indian-American girl in the world. At night, she dreamed up all kinds of romantic comedies, written by and starring someone just like her.

After school, Mindy would go to her mother's office and wait for her to finish work. Sometimes she took a book. At other times, she wrote her own scripts. Mindy was determined to become a comedy writer!

Doing some research, Mindy discovered that she could learn all the tricks of the trade at one place: college.

At that time, she also noticed that there were very few women working as comedy writers.

Mindy wrote for the college humor magazine, drew
a comic strip for the student newspaper, sang in an
a cappella group, and was a member of the improv team.
And she still found time to graduate as a playwright!

She was performing at a comedy club when she realized the MC had trouble pronouncing her last name. Mindy decided to change it to Kaling, which you can spot in the middle of her original last name, Chokalingam.

With her friend Brenda, she wrote a play about two famous actors that became a hit. The producer of a sitcom called 'The Office' went to see the show. Mindy's jokes were so hilarious that he decided to take a chance on her.

Mindy became one of the first women in 'The Office' writers' room... and she wrote some of the best dialogue. Soon, she was also playing a witty character called Kelly Kapoor.

Kelly was the main reason viewers looked forward to the next season of the show.

'The Office' was a big success and Mindy became a celebrity. But, there was so much more she wanted to do!

After six years of writing and producing, she become the first Indian-American woman to create and start her own show.

People found it refreshing to see Mindy Lahiri, an Indian doctor, as the star of a sitcom.

Still, Mindy wanted them to look at her just as she was:
a bubbly character with a great sense of humor.

So, whether she's producing sitcoms, creating comedies, directing shows, or writing books, Mindy is always doing what she loves most: telling stories. Especially for Mindy's favorite audience... her children.

And by breaking barriers and succeeding in the world of entertainment, little Mindy has become one of the world's most famous comedians—and a role model not just for other children, but also for herself.

MINDY KALING

(Born 1979)

2006

2017

Vera Mindy Chokalingam was born in Cambridge, Massachusetts, to an architect father and doctor mother, who met while working in a hospital together in Nigeria. Emigrating to the United States in the year before she was born, her parents gave her the nickname 'Mindy' while she was still in her mother's tummy. Her family home was a happy one, and from an early age, Mindy wanted to make people laugh—just like her parents did. At college, she involved herself in all areas of life: music, writing, comedy... and learning. She graduated in 2001 and moved to Brooklyn, New York. Working as a production assistant, she spent her evenings performing stand-up comedy in clubs across the city. Spotted for her ability to write original dialogue, she went to work on the award-winning BBC series

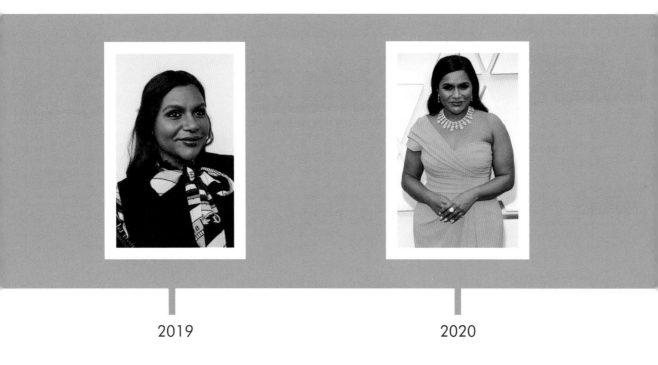

2019   2020

'The Office', adapting it for a North American audience. She was the only woman in a team of eight writers, and starred in one of the lead acting roles in the series. After winning five Emmys for her work, she went on to produce a single-camera series called 'The Mindy Project'. One of the world's first Indian-American women on camera, she was also a pioneer in how women were written into scripts, ensuring that female characters were just as complex as their male counterparts. She has gone on to write, produce, and star in more than 30 films and television series, bringing her quirky, bubbling humor to everyday moments and becoming a role model for South Asian women in Hollywood. Today, she lives and works in Los Angeles and has two young children... who also love to laugh!

Want to find out more about **Mindy Kaling?**

Have a read of these great books:

Stories for South Asian Supergirls by Raj Kaur Khaira

The Office: A Day at Dunder Mifflin Elementary by Robb Pearlman

Brimming with creative inspiration, how-to projects, and useful information to enrich your everyday life, Quarto Knows is a favourite destination for those pursuing their interests and passions. Visit our site and dig deeper with our books into your area of interest: Quarto Creates, Quarto Cooks, Quarto Homes, Quarto Lives, Quarto Drives, Quarto Explores, Quarto Gifts, or Quarto Kids.

Text © 2021 Maria Isabel Sánchez Vegara. Illustrations © 2021 Roza Nozari.

Original concept of the series by Maria Isabel Sánchez Vegara, published by Alba Editorial, s.l.u

Little People Big Dreams and Pequeña&Grande are registered trademarks of Alba Editorial, s.l.u. for books, printed publications, e-books and audiobooks.

Produced under licence from Alba Editorial, s.l.u.

First Published in the USA in 2021 by Frances Lincoln Children's Books, an imprint of The Quarto Group.

Quarto Boston North Shore, 100 Cummings Center, Suite 265D, Beverly, MA 01915, USA

Tel: +1 978-282-9590, Fax: +1 978-283-2742 **www.QuartoKnows.com**

ISBN 978-0-7112-5926-3

Set in Futura BT.

Published by Katie Cotton • Designed by Sasha Moxon

Edited by Katy Flint • Production by Nikki Ingram

Editorial Assistance from Alex Hithersay • Georgina Kamsika

Manufactured In China CC042021

1 3 5 7 9 8 6 4 2

Photographic acknowledgements (pages 28-29, from left to right): 1. Mindy Kaling as Kelly Kapoor, 2006 © Mitchell Haaseth/NBCU Photo Bank/NBCUniversal via Getty Images. 2. Mindy Kaling in 'Is That All There Is?', 2017 © Jordin Althaus/Hulu/courtesy Everett Collection. 3. Mindy Kaling from 'Late Night' poses for a portrait in the Pizza Hut Lounge in Park City, Utah on January 25, 2019 © Aaron Richter/Contour for Pizza Hut. 4. Mindy Kaling attends the 92nd Annual Academy Awards at Hollywood and Highland on February 09, 2020 in Hollywood, California. © Kevin Mazur/Getty Images.

Collect the *Little People,* **BIG DREAMS**™ series:

FRIDA KAHLO

COCO CHANEL

MAYA ANGELOU

AMELIA EARHART

AGATHA CHRISTIE

MARIE CURIE

ROSA PARKS

DREY HEPBURN

EMMELINE PANKHURST

ELLA FITZGERALD

ADA LOVELACE

JANE AUSTEN

GEORGIA O'KEEFFE

HARRIET TUBMAN

ANNE FRANK

MOTHER TERESA

JOSEPHINE BAKER

L. M. MONTGOMERY

JANE GOODALL

SIMONE DE BEAUVOIR

MUHAMMAD ALI

EPHEN HAWKING

MARIA MONTESSORI

VIVIENNE WESTWOOD

MAHATMA GANDHI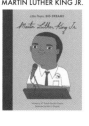

DAVID BOWIE

WILMA RUDOLPH

DOLLY PARTON

BRUCE LEE

RUDOLF NUREYEV

ZAHA HADID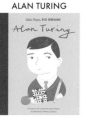

MARY SHELLEY

MARTIN LUTHER KING JR.

DAVID ATTENBOROUGH

ASTRID LINDGREN

ONNE GOOLAGONG

BOB DYLAN

ALAN TURING

BILLIE JEAN KING

GRETA THUNBERG

JESSE OWENS

JEAN-MICHEL BASQUIAT

ARETHA FRANKLIN

CORAZON AQUINO

PELÉ

ERNEST SHACKLETON

STEVE JOBS

AYRTON SENNA

LOUISE BOURGEOIS

ELTON JOHN

JOHN LENNON

PRINCE

CHARLES DARWIN

CAPTAIN TOM MOORE

HANS CHRISTIAN ANDERSEN

STEVIE WONDER

MEGAN RAPINOE

MARY ANNING

MALALA YOUSAFZAI

ANDY WARHOL
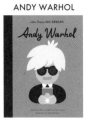

RUPAUL

MICHELLE OBAMA

MINDY KALING

IRIS APFEL

ROSALIND FRANKLIN

ACTIVITY BOOKS

STICKER ACTIVITY BOOK

COLORING BOOK

LITTLE ME, BIG DREAMS JOURNAL

Discover more about the series at www.littlepeoplebigdreams.com